Hardworking Cats

Hardworking Cats

A Humorous Look at the Feline Contribution to Our Workaday World

Written by Lisa Kerber
Illustrated by John Ungar

Skyhorse
Publishing

Library of Congress Cataloging-in-Publication Data is available on file.

Cover design by John Ungar
Cover illustration credit John Ungar

Print ISBN: 978-1-62914-704-8
Ebook ISBN: 978-1-62914-979-0

Printed in the United States of America

Dedicated to the many endearing personalities
who've worked so hard for us over the years:

Shu-Shu-La-Rue, Hot Helen, Boocat, Pickle, Hodge, Maui Moo,
Tudor, Chucky, Johnny, Posh, Peebzo, Lulu, Izzy, Ummie, and
the greatest of all: Rooney Toon and Wooodie the Woo.

Also, many thanks to Kelsie Besaw at Skyhorse for
her diligence, dedication, and enthusiasm in bringing
this book to life.

Thanks for all the jobs well done!

ARE CATS _REALLY_ AS LAZY AS SOME PEOPLE SAY? *Hmmm . . .*

Let's admit it . . . when cat lovers look fondly at our favorite felines, our first thought isn't how industrious they are.

It's more along the lines of, "How great you look with nicely combed fur," or "How cute you are meditating all day," or "How funny you are with that ping-pong ball."

So . . . we appreciate our furry little friends for lots of reasons. Companionship—yes! Lowering our blood pressure? Right! Warming our laps? Sure. Making us laugh? Of course!

But . . . gosh . . . we may get a little defensive when ordinary people ask, "What are cats good for anyway? All they do is sleep all day, eat expensive food, and rip up the furniture. Most don't even have the get-up-and-go to catch mice anymore!"

And sheepishly, we admit to ourselves some of that is true. Maybe, deep down, we're a little jealous of how cats get to sleep in on days when everyone else is dealing with the dog-eat-dog world. Perhaps we secretly envy their privileged lifestyle that comes with dedicated waiters and waitresses.

So, to answer the critics and justify our unfailing devotion to these little characters, we decided to look at cats in a whole new way. We wanted to see if our society's focus on the puritan work ethic had any effect on them at all.

And lo and behold, it turns out cats are doing way more than anyone imagined! With a little thinking outside the litter box, we came up with all sorts of ways cats contribute to the work-a-day world.

*In fact, we discovered 100 jobs
cats have been doing all along.*

So, cat parents, be proud! Read on! Celebrate
your favorite feline's rightful place in this modern
twenty-four-hour-a-day rat race. Ignore those
irksome skeptics and their dogmatic opinions.

And then add up your cat's total score at the
end of this book to see just how much he or she
matters—to us all!

Wake-Up Caller

Periodically checks to determine if sleeping humans know what time it is. Urgency of visits often depends on how long a certain food dish has been empty.

Official Greeter

Eagerly hightails it over to welcome anyone who drops by to visit the staff. Hangs around hoping for chin rubs, pats on the back, and compliments on charisma.

Hygienist

Dedicated to spiffing up every few hours, including the top of one's head, even though there's no way to see up there.

Courier

Heads off youthful misadventures by returning errant offspring to their rightful positions. Favors old-fashioned method of parenting involving the scruff of the neck.

Exterminator

Skillfully dispatches any creature that scurries, flies,
or offends humans. Job performance of this classic
feline tradition may be hampered by a big dinner.

Interior Decorator

Easily becomes bored with neatness and order. Shows artistic flair by pushing paper, pens, or jewelry onto the floor to liven up the place.

Wilderness Explorer

Enjoys exciting expeditions into woods, gardens, and fields. When lost in the moment, may need some verbal assistance to find the way home.

Sunspot Researcher

Looks for sunny rectangles on floors, and monitors the BTUs until the spot moves away. Work may continue elsewhere if research gets too hot to handle.

Investigator

Likes to check out every intriguing space.
New discoveries are kept in mind in case of
the need to disappear for awhile.

Lookout

Spends endless hours surveying the view outside,
with occasional astonished looks, alert posture, and
low growls if one's territory is invaded.

Black-Hole Researcher

Stares for hours at dark openings in the ground waiting for something exciting to pop up. Success depends on figuring out which hole to watch.

Furniture Stripper

Skilled at deupholstering couches and chairs so humans
can have fun picking out new fabrics and patterns. If scolded
too often, may switch to the night shift to avoid interruptions.

Comedian

Likes to perform funny antics to make humans laugh. Knows everyone enjoys a little bathroom humor now and then.

Bookkeeper

Loves books ... as long as enough are pushed together
to make room for a nap. Such literary pursuits may
lead to a dream job as a bookstore's resident mascot.

Curtain Hanger

Can't resist the thrill of a vertical climb ending with a great view. However, snags in the fabric may lead to human tantrums.

Diplomat

Cozies up to one's enemies, especially since it's the only way to keep them from eating your lunch. Diversity training helpful.

Food Critic

Uses sniff tests to judge meals offered by the staff.
Often picky, insisting on the world's highest standard
of culinary excellence—Feline Grade AAA+.

Night Watchman

Enjoys working third shift with dilated pupils
as night vision goggles. Skilled at nabbing
fleet-footed trespassers.

Teacher

Maintains eternal patience while giving lessons on
how to stay well groomed, act cool, and be endearing
to humans—all beneficial to future employability.

Trash Collector

Good at finding wads of paper to scoot across the
floor during games of field hockey. Considers every
wastebasket a source of mystery and fun.

Dog Trainer

Understands the psychology of happy-go-lucky canine
companions, and reminds them to respect their superiors.
May use quick bops to establish who's really the boss.

Yoga Practitioner

Prefers stretching poses, especially after long naps.
Understandably, tends to avoid the position
downward-facing dog.

Job Supervisor

Likes to sit near human workers to monitor their progress and ensure jobs are done properly. Frequent breaks are taken if supervision becomes too boring.

Data Entry Typist

Enjoys the springy feeling of a keyboard while putting
secret messages on a screen. Thinks it's fun to hold down
certain keys, leaving humans to figure out who wrote:
sssssssffffhhhjjjjjmmmmm.

Quick Change Artist

Has fickle mood swings from cool to crazed to everything in between. Often changes mind about whether to go outside or stay in or come back inside or stay out.

Daredevil

Loves the challenge of steep ascents, but needs to be creative in getting down without help from a fire department.

Masseuse

Skilled in walking up and down on sleeping humans.
Advanced level includes steady kneading on one spot.
Not recommended: massages before the alarm goes off.

Bureaucrat

Keeps an eye out for open drawers suitable for a
cozy snooze. Stays alert for humans who might
try to close one while a nap is underway.

Cave Explorer

Likes to check for boogeymen in dark places.
Related tasks include dusting behind furniture
with whiskers and ear tips.

JOB № 31

Censor

Has an uncanny ability to figure out which paragraph
a human is reading and then sit on it to get attention.
This talent is especially handy when dinner is overdue.

Peace Activist

Makes good-faith efforts to pal around with local canines.
If not successful, reverts to Job #22 (Dog Trainer) or
Job #77 (Sprinter).

Flower Arranger

Sometimes gets an urge to push flower pots onto the
floor just to see what happens. Colorful arrangements
and broken vases are considered feline art.

Reconnaissance Expert

Keeps an eye out for humans who might disrupt
a pleasant day, especially if they're carrying a pill
popper, nail clipper, or tiny toothbrush.

Mattress Evaluator

Eagerly volunteers to assess beds for snooze worthiness.
While conducting tests, also serves as a bed warmer
and nice touch to the room's decor.

Featherweight Wrestler

Has fun tussling with feline friends to amuse human
sports fans. Each match typically ends in a draw,
followed by a less stressful pursuit like snack time.

Entertainer

Enjoys performing hijinks to get humans to watch, smile, and laugh. Success depends on how often they tell friends about funniest stunts.

Therapist

Good at figuring out when friends could use some moral support and quality time. Gentle head bumps, purring, and warm raspy kisses help make things better.

Herbalist

Finds certain aromatic plants irresistible. Frivolity often follows due to performance-enhancing drugs. Humans will be amused by this.

Sleep Researcher

Seeks to answer the question: "Is it possible to be conked out twenty-four hours a day?" Experiments with each position of slumber—the Cannonball, the Flopover, the String Bean, the Sphinx, and the always amusing Belly Up.

Skydiver

Remains fearless when making great leaps of faith
from one point to another. Ideally, landings
should be mapped out before takeoffs.

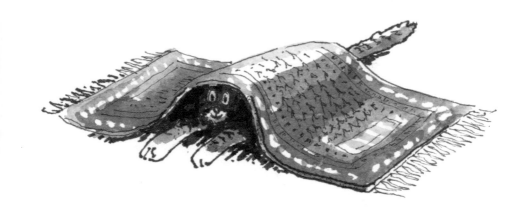

Tunnel Surveyor

Likes to check out narrow spaces that provide a tight fit and some light at the end. New discoveries become hideouts or fun places to zoom through.

Plumbing Inspector

Bravely investigates all sources of moving water,
no matter where it's found . . .

Ex-Plumbing Inspector

. . . certain pitfalls aside, of course.

Music Critic

Quickly determines which selections are suitable
for refined tastes and which aren't. Negative reviews
are expressed by flattened ears and hasty exits.

Grass Cutter

Likes to enjoy a savory salad during excursions outdoors,
although unfortunate choices may lead to an abrupt
reversal of fortune (see Job #71).

Actor

Pretends there was no involvement in whatever
just went wrong. Talented at playing the role
of wayward innocent.

Heating Expert

Carefully researches the warmest, coziest spot in
the house, and then claims it for the winter.

Paper Pusher

Likes to keep desktops free of clutter. When enough pieces of paper wind up on the floor, it's time for a game of slip 'n slide.

Sanitation Engineer

Very fastidious about personal hygiene and making
sure nothing unpleasant sees the light of day.
Shallow digging required.

Supermodel

Attends family photo sessions and tends to ignore requests to look at the camera. Acts as if all the attention is well deserved.

Ornithologist

Focuses like a laser on how birds flutter, hop, and chirp.
A little feline chattering helps vent frustrations.
Snagging subjects for close-up study greatly discouraged.

Ichthyologist

Spends hours studying how fish live happily in
an unpleasant substance. May tap the glass now
and then to keep things moving.

Fisherman

Able to overcome disdain for wetness to achieve one's goals. Eternal optimism helps since targets are elusive.

Organic Gardener

Assists master gardeners in fertilizing flower beds without chemicals. Requires some earth moving experience.

Relaxation Coach

Shows mastery of positions for Purposeful Resting.
Offers daily demonstrations of how these ancient techniques
lead to the highest levels of contentment.

Hairstylist

Good at grooming mussed-up fur into the latest style—slicked down. When done, each client's coat has been cleaned and smoothed with a damp comb.

Pianist

Offers impromptu compositions of modern music to impress friends. Each selection is always unique and limited to four notes at a time.

Patrol Officer

Takes daily strolls around the neighborhood to check
for trespassers. Any suspicious characters scurrying
around may be hauled in for questioning.

Movie Reviewer

Watches new cat videos to see if the performances are any good. Positive reviews are expressed by wide-eyed stares and vivid commentary on the feathered and furry actors.

Pants Presser

Spends hours trying to flatten clothing creases on laps. Permanent press garments may require overtime.

Ballplayer

Loves to keep round objects in motion. After the final ping-pong ball disappears under the couch, it's fun to see how much yarn can be unraveled before yelling begins.

JOB № 63

Undercover Agent

Studies the hang of bedspreads to find an entryway to
a pleasant snooze. Trusts that humans will notice the
lump on the bed before lying down.

Beauty Queen

Must have gorgeous eyes, dainty nose, and a fabulous fur coat to be a glamour-puss. Doesn't need makeup and should do own hair.

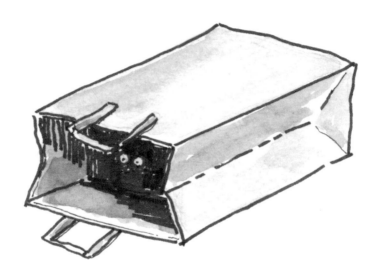

Grocery Bag Recycler

Thinks it's fun to reuse paper bags as hangouts or campsites as long as human friends don't accidentally pick up a bag while occupied.

Roving Ambassador

Enjoys visiting nearby houses to schmooze with occupants. Keeps track of which neighbors provide the best face rubs and tasty treats.

Adventurer

Can't resist the lure of unexplored rooftops, especially if a ladder is left up overnight. This derring-do attitude often leads to lofty predicaments.

Arborist

Uses retractable tree spikes to climb up and explore nearby treetops. Finds the trip down calls for critical analysis and some reverse psychology.

Caregiver

Likes to spend quality time with soul mates sitting around and enjoying quiet moments. Prefers friends with common interests such as the love of naps.

Furniture Polisher

Feels compelled to shine wooden furniture legs
now and then. Provides own buffing pad, and
wets it down frequently.

Casting Director

Has a firm sense of what to do when things are not
going well. Tosses out whatever isn't quite right.

Entomologist

Fascinated by any creature with more than four legs.
Preemptive bops help determine if a sting or bite
poses a threat to research.

Carpet Tester

Routinely rakes carpeting to see if the weave is holding true. If fibers pull out, the bare backing lets humans know to buy better next time.

Babysitter

Keeps tabs on little fuzzballs who are either asleep
or getting in trouble. Must accept job hazards of
messed up fur, nibbled ears, and chewed tail.

Gourmet

Evaluates each offering for taste, aroma, and whether the price is high enough. Approvals are based on epicurean judgment or time since the latest snack.

Dishwasher

Ensures plates and bowls are squeaky clean, especially
of tasty gravy. When done properly, dishes are polished and
ready for the cupboard. Or not.

Sprinter

Can propel oneself to full speed in seconds, especially if things go wrong on the diplomatic front. Stays alert for local bullies, with a last-ditch resort to using sharp body parts for defense.

Meditation Guru

Assumes upright position with eyes closed and legs tucked
under while mulling over big issues, such as what's for dinner
and how to get another neck rub.

Tree Trimmer

Inspects any tree that suddenly appears indoors, which tends to happen once a year. May learn the hard way that some are not what they seem.

Naturalist

Likes to study insects, amphibians, reptiles, birds, mammals, and rustling leaves. On slow days, may stay in practice by staring intensely at nothing.

Nurse

Willing to serve as a milk bar for overstimulated
fun seekers who need an energy drink. Also may
double as a hairstylist to pass the time.

Toy Tester

Analyzes whether new offerings that twirl, flutter, wiggle, or roll are worthy of limited energy reserves. Approvals tend to go down as age goes up.

JOB № 83

Advertising Director

Never misses an opportunity to let everyone know
who owns the neighborhood. However, placing the
same spritzed message indoors may lead to eviction.

Vocalist

Offers colorful vocal commentary to human, feline, and canine friends. May also perform serenades outdoors if the nightlife needs to be jazzed up.

Ommmmm

Purrrrr

Zen Master

Shows mastery of mantras by prolonged purring,
thereby elevating oneself to the highest level of
relaxed consciousness. Napping nirvana often follows.

Child Surrogate

Soaks up the parental pampering typically lavished on the smallest member of the family. Often good at acting out the lyrics of "Be My Baby."

Travel Critic

Expresses strong opinions about being locked in a box inside a moving object. Commentary often continues while in transit. Prefers to stay home during family vacations with a helpful neighbor as butler.

Public Relations Expert

Adept at purring, slow blinks, friendly conversation, head bumps, ankle rubbing, lap sitting, and other charming behavior. When successful, enjoys lifetime employment.

Hunter

Specializes in fast pursuits and quick grabs—even when success is elusive. Doesn't mind if a moving target turns out to be a fake, since it's all just for sport anyway.

Clown

Puts a humorous spin on whatever might be good for laughs. Knows flying leaps and mid-air twists are always crowd pleasers.

Sidekick

Enjoys hanging around with humans who appreciate
the feline way of life. Likes to keep track of what they're
up to, with friendship confirmed by time spent together.

Doorman

Easily opens doors when the staff doesn't cooperate.
Prefers hooking and pulling, but also knows a big shove
makes for a grand entrance. Closing skills not required, since
felines see no purpose in this.

Printmaker

Expresses creativity by using muddy paws to decorate cars, which amuses strangers who see a traveling art show go by.

Website Manager

Monitors local networks of any web that needs periodic attention. Going worldwide not required.

Acrobat

Shows off athletic talents by gracefully defying gravity.
Performances last only a few minutes before calling it
a day . . . or two or three.

Storm Forecaster

At the first hint of thunder, heads for a safe haven just in case a monster might be outside. Afterward, pretends like nothing happened.

Contortionist

Skilled at twisting oneself into unnatural positions
to take care of personal hygiene. Resistance training
may be a bonus.

Escape Artist

Plans out strategic retreats in advance, and then
takes action when faced with certain loud guests,
canines, or too much commotion.

Go Getter

Has mastered the time honored feline technique of
going to get a favorite human, demanding attention,
and leading them to a door to be opened or dish to
be filled.

Philosopher

Likes to endlessly ponder the Big Questions of feline life such as, "Who turns off the sun at night?" and "Why must there be dogs in the world?" The energy required for this deep thinking often leads to the need for naps.

And the No. 1 job is . . .

Homemaker

Happily schmoozes . . . pals around . . . strikes classic poses . . .
entertains . . . and offers daily demonstrations of how to enjoy
the good life. All essential to making a house a home!

So . . . cats actually do more than we first thought! To see for yourself, go back and count all the job skills of your favorite felines. Then use the ranking below to figure out what to offer for a compensation package. And be sure to give them the benefit of any doubts—they deserve it!

51+ jobs: Wow, your overachiever deserves a nice relaxing vacation with lots of pricey meals.

31–50 jobs: Very impressive and worthy of plenty of extra back rubs and neck massages.

16–30 jobs: Certainly making a good effort, and deserves hours of petting followed by some toe tickles.

Up to 15 jobs: Still making a valuable contribution, but may be devoting some time to philosophizing about how wonderful it is to live with you.